MATERIALS

EXTREME FACTS

BY ROBIN TWIDDY

©2019
The Secret Book Company
King's Lynn
Norfolk PE30 4LS

ISBN: 978-1-912502-27-1

Printed in Malaysia

Written by:
Robin Twiddy
Edited by:
Madeline Tyler
Designed by:
Jasmine Pointer

A catalogue record for this book is available from the British Library

All facts, statistics, web addresses and URLs in this book were verified as valid and accurate at time of writing. No responsibility for any changes to external websites or references can be accepted by either the author or publisher.

PHOTO CREDITS

Front cover – 32 pixels, Aurora72, intararit, MicroOne, LynxVector, SVPanteon. 4 – Migren art, Laia Design Lab, BigMouse, BATKA, denk creative. 5 – Maksim M, tmicons, Humdan, Ilya Bolotov, Mykhailo Bokovan. 6 – O39I , Gennadii Korchuganov, Golden Sikorka, MSSA, lady-luck, Danielle Jones. 7 – Magicleaf, lukpedclub, MuchMania, ArnyGFX. 8 – Sunnydream, boykung, BlueRingMedia, Rvector, Macrovector, Boyko.Pictures. 9 – TatianaKost94, Sunflowerr, azurel, Elizaveta Melentyeva, Graphic Treasure, T. Lesia. 10 – GraphicsRF, Panda Vector, DECTER. 11 – Jemastock, DRogatnev, Macrovector. 12 – Natali Snailcat, Dukesn, Orakunya, Supriya07. 13 – Ysami, VikiVector, Kaleo, Enmaler, Katy Flaty, grmarc. 14 – Macrovector, Comscreen, Forgem. 15 – konstantinks, Looper, Social Media hub, Luis Molinero. 16 – NotionPic, hvostik, Tomacco, Baurz1973, robuart. 17 – NPavelN, matsabe, xio3, naum. 18 – NotionPic, hvostik, Tomacco, Baurz1973, robuart. 19 – Anatolir, Jennifer Wallace, Gaidamashchuk, Chalintra.B, hvostiK, turbo_turbo. 20 – PremiumArt. Marnikus, Agor2012, Miyu Nur. 21 – MatiasDelCarmine, GarikProst, Inna Bigun, Pablo Prat. 22 – Nadia Snopek, Alena Nv. 23 – Panda Vector, Design tech art, Iconic Bestiar.

Images are courtesy of Shutterstock.com. With thanks to Getty Images, Thinkstock Photo and iStockphoto.

CONTENTS

Words that look like this can be found in the glossary on page 24.

MEASURING MATERIALS

Here are some ways of measuring materials that might help you to understand some of the facts better.

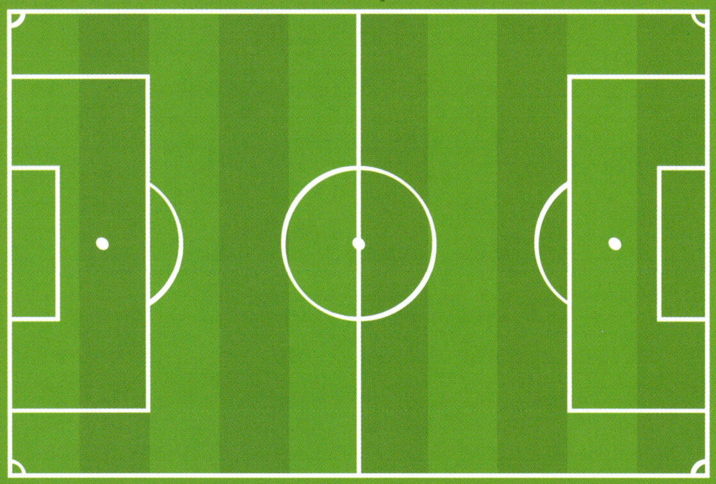

Square metres is a measurement used to measure rooms, houses and large spaces. One square metre is a square where each side is one metre long. The average professional football pitch is 7,140 square metres.

A gram is a measurement of weight. A paperclip is about one gram and a small **bag of sugar** is around 453 grams.

Carats are used to measure the purity of gold. **Pure gold is 24 carats.**

Tonnes are used to measure the weight of really heavy things. One tonne is about as heavy as one and a half cows.

The Mohs scale of hardness measures how hard a mineral is by seeing which of the ten minerals on the scale can scratch it. The softest mineral on the scale is talc and the hardest is diamond.

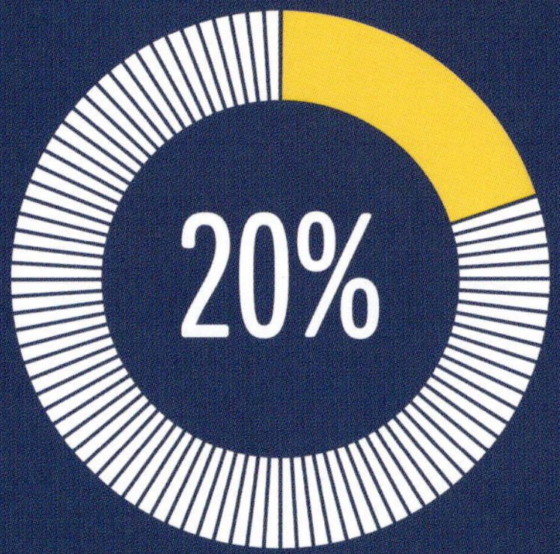

When thinking about a **percentage**, imagine that a whole thing has been split into 100 pieces. If we are talking about something that is 20 percent (%), it is 20 of those 100 pieces.

PSI is short for pounds per square inch. It is a measurement of pressure. It can be used to measure air in a bike tyre or the pressure of a heavy object on another object.

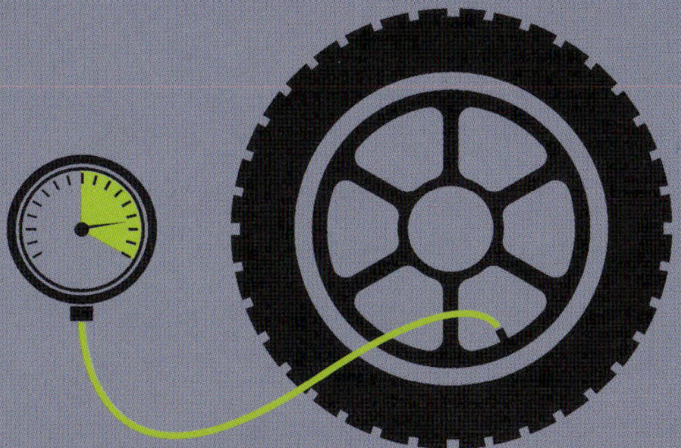

You can come back to these pages at any time!

EXTREME BUILDING MATERIALS

ICEHOTEL in Jukkasjärvi, Sweden, was the first hotel to be built from **snow and ice.** It covers around 5,500 square metres.

Believe it or not, lots of people have used old **shipping containers** to build homes!

Bricks can be made from **mushrooms!** Plant waste is put into a brick-shaped mould. Then mycelium, the root-like fibres of mushrooms, grow through it, binding it into a brick.

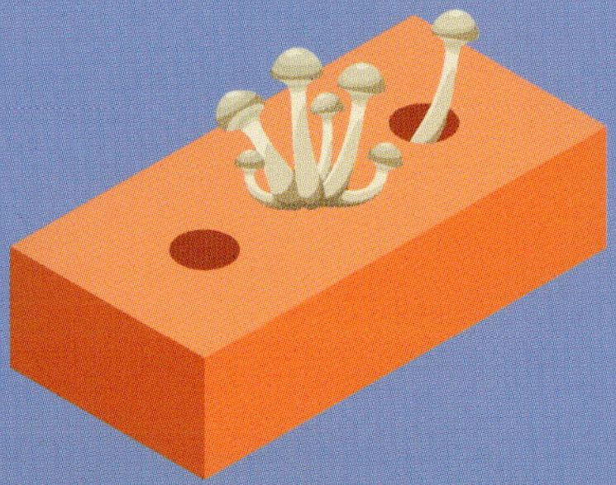

The world's oldest building material is compressed earth. This is when mud and dirt is squeezed really hard until it is solid. People were doing this over 5,000 years ago.

The world's largest Victorian greenhouse is in Kew Gardens in the UK. It has over **15,000** panes of glass.

Used nappies can be recycled into building materials. Recycling machines can take out the baby poo and turn the old nappies into tiles for the roofs of houses.

Newspaper wood is made from old, rolled-up newspaper that is glued to make logs. They are then cut into planks. Anything that you would normally make from wood can be made from newspaper **wood**.

The Great Wall of China is held together with a material made from sticky rice!

FABRIC

Cotton is stronger when it is wet.

Flax is a plant that is used to make a material called linen. It was first used over 7,000 years ago.

The cocoon of the silkworm is made from a single silk thread that can reach up to one kilometre in length.

It takes over 2,000 silkworm cocoons to produce enough silk to make a single kimono.

Jeans get their name from the word Gênes, the French name for the Italian city Genoa, that the material comes from.

The world's longest wedding dress train is 8,095.40 meters.

Would you wear trousers made from slime? The hagfish releases slime to protect it from predators. This slime contains strong fibres. Scientists believe that this could be the next big thing in fabrics.

A new fabric has been invented using fibres from stinging nettles. Don't worry – it isn't itchy!

The world's oldest trousers were found in China. They were made of wool and had been buried for over 3,000 years.

EXTREMELY RARE

Materials that are hard to find are known as rare materials. These rare materials are usually worth more money. Here are some of the rarest materials on Earth.

Gold: All the gold that has ever been found would fit in a square box with 25-metre-long sides.

Platinum: Platinum is even rarer than gold. For every 400 grams of gold that is mined, only 28 grams of platinum is mined.

Red Beryl: Red beryl is a very rare stone. It is believed that only one crystal of red beryl is found for every 150,000 good-quality diamonds that are found.

Painite: Painite is one of the rarest minerals on Earth, and one of the hardest to find. It can only be found in Myanmar.

Plutonium: Plutonium can be found naturally on Earth, but it is very rare. Almost all plutonium is made by humans in nuclear power plants.

Californium: Californium can only be made in a laboratory. It is very expensive and costs over 20 million pounds per gram.

PLASTIC

Plastic doesn't biodegrade. It just breaks down into smaller pieces of plastic.

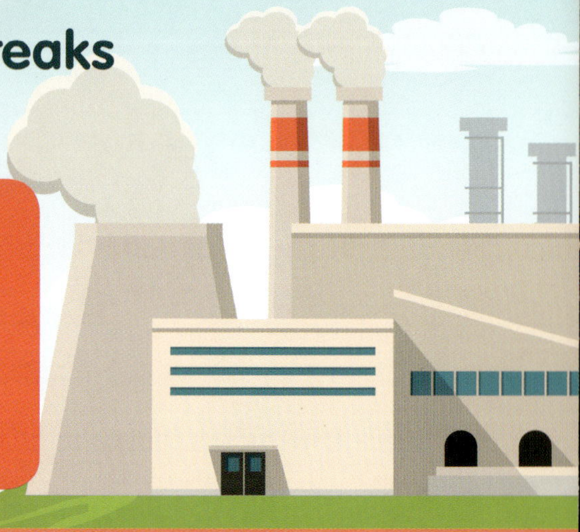

In 1990, around 90 million tonnes of plastic were produced around the world. In 2015, over 290 million tonnes were produced worldwide.

Around 7.5 billion tonnes of plastic have been made worldwide since the 1950s.

Only 9% of this plastic has been recycled.

Around 1 million seabirds and 100,000 sea mammals are killed each year because they swallow plastic.

Here are some surprising places that you can find plastic in your home…

Plastic is used to close tea bags!

Most chewing gum contains plastic.

Drink cans contain a thin layer of plastic. Without it, fizzy drinks would eat through the metal of the can.

Lots of clothes contain plastic fibres.

Drink cartons for chocolate milk, orange juice and other drinks contain a layer of plastic.

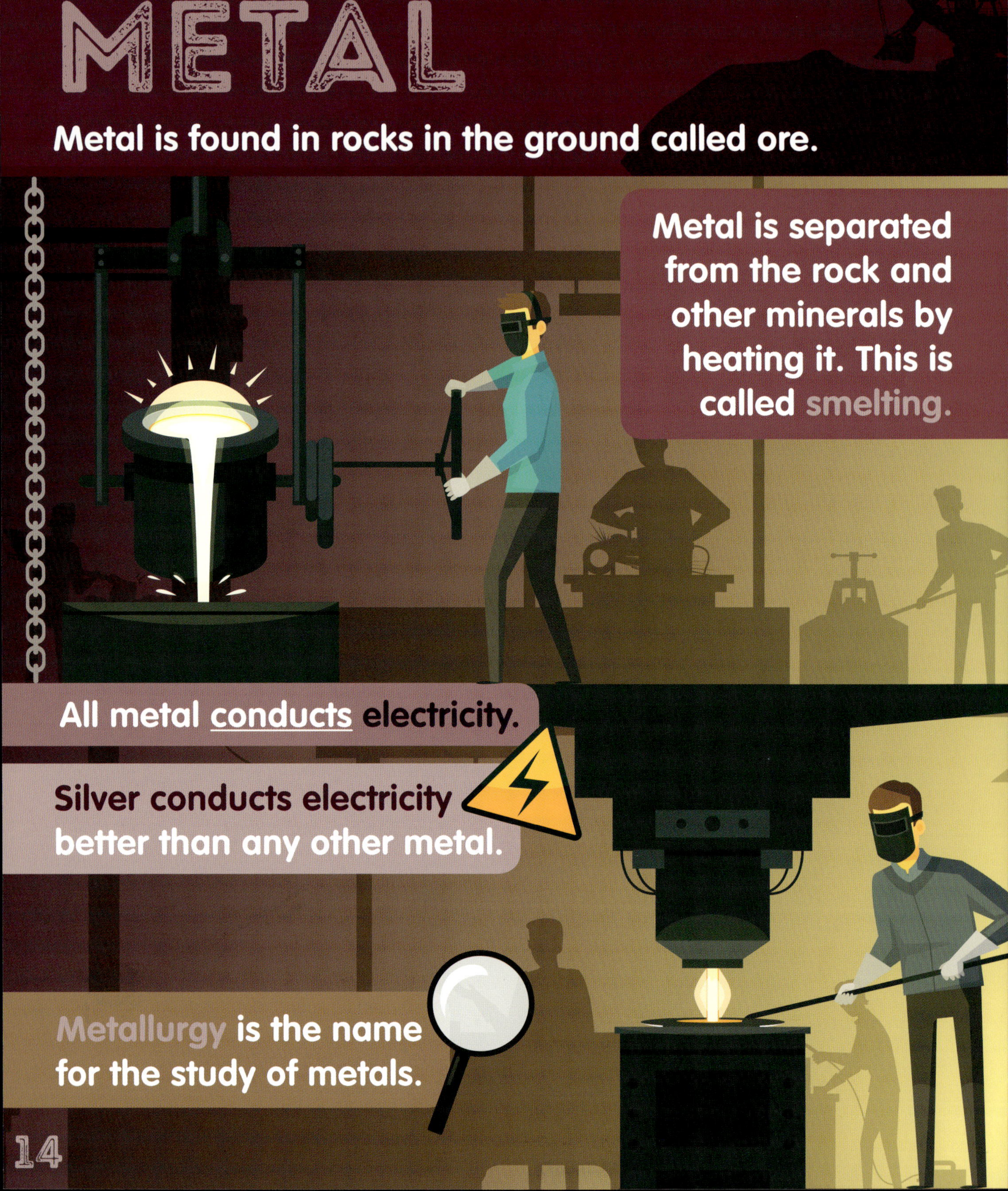

METAL

Metal is found in rocks in the ground called ore.

Metal is separated from the rock and other minerals by heating it. This is called smelting.

All metal conducts electricity.

Silver conducts electricity better than any other metal.

Metallurgy is the name for the study of metals.

Chromium is the hardest of all metals on the Mohs scale of metal hardness.

There is more iron in the universe than any other metal.

Mercury has the lowest melting point of all metals. It becomes a liquid at room temperature – that's around 20 degrees Celsius (°C)!

The Eiffel Tower is about 15 centimetres taller in the summer than the winter. This is because the steel and iron it is made from <u>expand</u> when heated.

Brass and bronze naturally kill <u>bacteria</u>. This is why they are often used for handles and handrails.

DIAMONDS

The word diamond comes from the Greek word 'adamas', which means invincible.

The ancient Romans and ancient Greeks believed that diamonds were the tears of the gods.

The oldest diamond ever discovered is believed to be over 4 billion years old.

The graphite in your pencil is made from 100% carbon. Believe it or not, so are diamonds.

Diamonds have been found in meteorites that have crash-landed on Earth from outer space.

It takes extreme heat – over 1,090°C – and pressures of around 725,000 PSI to create diamonds.

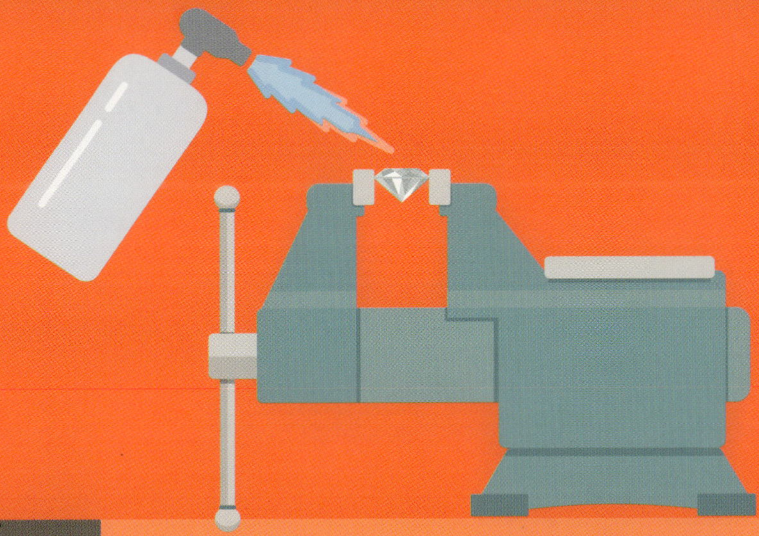

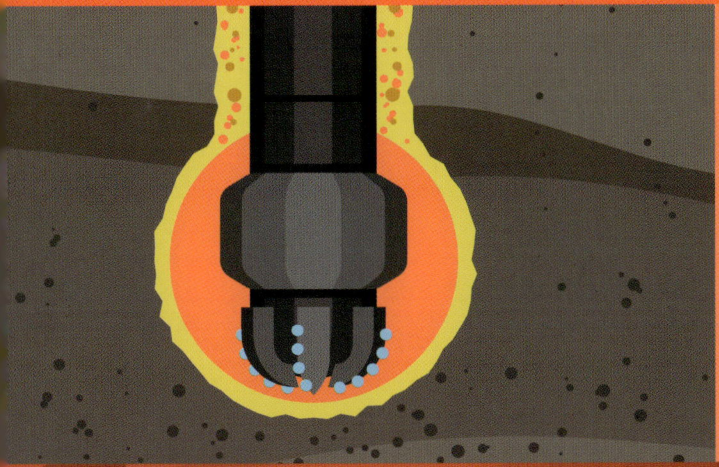

Around **80%** of all mined diamonds are used to make drill ends and other industrial equipment.

The largest diamond ever discovered is the Cullinan diamond at **3,106 carats.** That is 621 grams.

The ashes of a cremated body can be turned into a diamond! Because the human body has a large amount of carbon in it, it simply takes a lot of pressure and heat.

UNUSUAL ART MATERIALS

Maurice Bennett, a man from New Zealand, makes art from toast. He uses hundreds of pieces of burnt toast to make amazing pictures.

Artist Lin Evola-Smidt makes statues of angels from melted-down guns to protest against gun crime in New York.

Maurizio Savini makes amazing statues using bubble gum. Some are as large as a fully grown adult.

Some artists use a combination of rubbish and lights to create shadow sculptures.

ANIMAL ARCHITECTS

Spiders make their own building material called spider silk. It is used to build webs for homes and traps for their prey.

Fire ants use their own bodies as building materials to build bridges, boats and shelters!

Beavers build dams to block streams and make lakes. They then use logs and twigs to build their homes in the middle of the newly formed lake.

The **caddisfly** larvae builds its own cocoon using materials it can find on the ground such as sand, shells and pebbles. It ties it all together with the silk it produces. This gives it a tough suit of armour.

Trapdoor spiders use soil, plants and their own silk to build doors to their underground homes.

MATERIALS THAT ARE OUT OF THIS WORLD

Asteroids can contain lots of different metals. Some of these metals are:

- Iridium
- Nickle
- Palladium
- Magnesium
- Iron
- Platinum
- Gold

Scientists believe that in the future people will use special spaceships to mine asteroids for these materials.

Aluminium is one of the main materials used in spacecraft. This is because it is very strong and very light.

Astronaut Karen Nyberg sewed a small quilt whilst in space. She said that cutting, threading and sewing when weightless was very challenging.

The International Space Station (ISS) experiences extreme hot and cold temperatures as it moves closer to and farther away from the Sun. The materials used to make it need to be able to protect it from both.

Spacesuits are made from lots of different materials:

- Nylon tricot
- Spandex
- Polyester
- Neoprene
- Mylar
- Gortex
- Kevlar
- Nomex

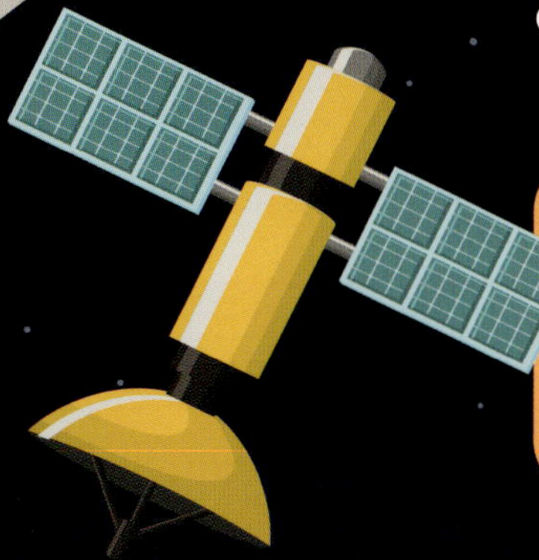

Satellites are covered in shiny sheets. These sheets look like gold, but they are actually made from plastic and aluminium.

In 1980, a meteorite crashed into the Earth in Yemen. It was made up of lots of different minerals. Some of these have never been found naturally on Earth.

MATERIALS OF THE FUTURE

Dutch scientists believe that mushrooms could be the material of the future. They have made chairs, lampshades and even slippers from mushrooms!

Scientists have been working on making an invisibility cloak. They would need to make a new material that can bend light around itself, making it invisible.

Aerogel is a new material with lots of strange properties. It is sometimes called frozen smoke because of how it looks. It is a great insulator and can keep you warm or cool.

Kaynemaile is completely recyclable and incredibly strong. It looks like chain mail and is being used to protect buildings and make them stronger.

Metal foam is super strong and super light. To make it, gas bubbles are added to liquid metal. It's strong enough to stop and shatter bullets!

Spider silk is very strong; scientists have made a version in the laboratory. It could be used for bullet-proof clothing, ropes, seatbelts and more!

Vantablack is a material made by humans that **absorbs 99.96% of light.** This makes it the darkest material known.

GLOSSARY

asteroids	small, rocky objects that orbit the Sun
bacteria	tiny living things that can cause diseases
biodegrade	to be broken down by bacteria or other living things
compressed	pressed or squeezed so that it becomes smaller or fills less space
conducts	lets electricity pass through it
cremated	having been burnt to ashes; usually a human body at a funeral
expand	become bigger
fibres	thread-like structures
insulator	a material that doesn't easily allow heat to travel through it
invincible	unbeatable
kimono	a traditional Japanese dress
laboratory	a room or building that has the technology needed to do scientific experiments
larvae	young insects that must grow and change before they reach their adult form
mammals	animals that are warm blooded, have a backbone and make milk to feed their young
mined	when something has been dug from the ground, usually minerals such as coal, gold and precious stones
mineral	a material formed in the earth that is not a plant or animal
nuclear power plants	power stations that collect energy from atoms, which are tiny things, too small to see, that make up everything
predators	animals that eat other animals for food
pressure	a force on an object caused by something pressing against it
prey	animals that are hunted by other animals for food
properties	physical qualities of a material
protest	to show you don't agree with something
recycled	used again to make something else
Victorian	of the time when Queen Victoria ruled England, from 1837 to 1901

INDEX